Our Garden in the City

Patterns

Rann Roberts

Publishing Credits

Dona Herweck Rice, *Editor-in-Chief*; Lee Aucoin, *Creative Director*; Don Tran, *Print Production Manager*; Sara Johnson, *Senior Editor*; Jamey Acosta, *Associate Editor*; Neri Garcia, *Interior Layout Designer*; Stephanie Reid, *Photo Editor*; Rachelle Cracchiolo, M.A.Ed., *Publisher*

Image Credits

cover Joe Klune/Laura Stone/Shutterstock; p.1 Joe Klune/Laura Stone/Shutterstock; p.4 Gorin/Shutterstock; p.5 Losevsky Pavel/Shutterstock; p.6 AMA/Shutterstock; p.7 Alex Garaev/Shutterstock; p.8 Agata Dorobek/Noam Armonn/Shutterstock; p.9 (top left) Nikita Tiunov/Shutterstock, (top right) Maslov Dmitry/Shutterstock, (bottom) Danylchenko Iaroslav/Shutterstock; p.10 tatianatatiana/iStockphoto; p.11 (top) Modesto Bee/Newscom, (bottom) Zuma Press/Newscom; p.12 Frances M. Roberts/Newscom; p.13 Newscast/Newscom; p.14 (top) Jeannie Long, (bottom) Daina Falk/Shutterstock; p.15 (top) Darryl Brooks/BigStockPhoto, (bottom) Andrew Chambers/BigStockPhoto; p.16 (top) Richard B. Levine/Newscom, (bottom) Scott Latham/Shutterstock; p.17 KRT/Newscom; p.18 Anna Ceglin´ska/Dreamstime; p.19 Supertrooper/VLDR/Lepas/Mashe/Shutterstock; p.20 Realistic Reflections; p.21 Tanya McConnell/BigStockPhoto; p.22 (left) YellowJ/Shutterstock, (right) Georgy Markov/Shutterstock; p.23 (top left) Ivaschenko Roman/Shutterstock, (top right) Witson/Dreamstime, (bottom) Ivaschenko Roman/Andrjuss/Shutterstock; p.24 (top) Clarence S. Lewis/Shutterstock, (bottom) Roslen Mack/Shutterstock; p.25 Craig Barhorst/Shutterstock; p.26 (top) Lisa F. Young/Shutterstock, (bottom) ALL/Newscom; p.27 Nikolay Stefanov Dimitrov/Shutterstock; p.28 James R. Martin/Shutterstock

Teacher Created Materials

5301 Oceanus Drive
Huntington Beach, CA 92649-1030
http://www.tcmpub.com
ISBN 978-0-7439-0867-2

Table of Contents

City Gardens

Many people live in cities. They may not have room for a garden. They may live in apartment buildings. They may live in a house with a small yard.

But people still like to eat fresh fruits and vegetables. And many people like to work in gardens and grow things.

Not having a yard does not stop some people from growing things. They may plant a few things in pots. They may put them on a balcony or deck. Some people may put them in **patterns**. Look at the picture below. What pattern do you see?

Some people live on the top floors of their buildings. They may make gardens on their roofs. Those people are lucky!

Many different types of plants can grow on rooftops. Trees and bushes can be planted in large pots. Vegetables and flowers can be planted in smaller pots or flower boxes.

LET'S EXPLORE MATH

A rooftop garden has bushes and trees. They are put in a pattern against the edge of the roof. The pattern looks like this:

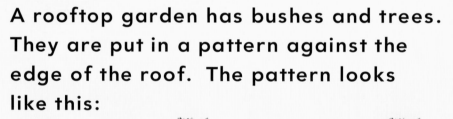

a. What type of plant would come next?

b. What type of plant would be 9th?

There is a lot of sunlight on rooftops, so plants grow well. Birds, butterflies, and bees may use the plants for food or shelter.

Making a City Garden

Some people do not have any room for a garden. So, the people who want a garden **organize** a team. Then they find an empty lot.

They get permission to use it for their garden. They plan how to clean it up and get rid of the trash. Then, they get to work.

Clean-Up Jobs

- recycling cans
- recycling bottles
- recycling paper
- removing concrete
- removing litter
- removing rocks
- stacking old bricks

The garden team meets to plan the space. They make a plan for small garden **plots**. There is also room for fruit trees, a **compost** area, and benches.

They make sure that they have access to water. Now they can let people plan their own gardens. Many people like to plant their gardens using patterns.

People can be very creative at recycling things found on the lot. They may use old bricks to make borders for the planting beds.

LET'S EXPLORE MATH

This is a pattern used for the walls of the planting beds.

a. What color brick comes next?

b. What is the color of the 14th brick?

They may also use old boards. People may even use ropes and stakes to mark each small garden area.

People may get donations of things such as soil and seeds. A lumber store may give wood for building a **shed**. The shed will store things such as rakes and shovels.

It is important to have supplies for watering the plants. People may use watering cans or hoses. They may even be able to set up a **drip irrigation system**. This will help save water.

All Kinds of Gardens

Sometimes a garden team plants small fruit trees first. They choose these small trees for 2 reasons. They take up the least space. And they will have lots of fruit to share in just 2 or 3 years.

Some teams plant spring **crops** in their planting beds. Vegetables such as cabbage, carrots, celery, and broccoli grow well in cool spring weather.

cabbage   celery   carrots   broccoli

LET'S EXPLORE MATH

One family plants cabbage, carrots, celery, and broccoli. They start with a row of cabbage. They plant carrots in the next row. They plant celery in the third row. In the fourth row they plant broccoli.

cabbage   carrots   celery   **broccoli**

a. If they continue this pattern, what will they plant in the next row?

b. If they continue this pattern, what will they plant in the 8th row?

Many people like to plant flowers. Beautiful patterns can be made with flowers.

This garden has many flowers. The rows form a color pattern.

LET'S EXPLORE MATH

The chart below shows how much it costs to buy small flowers at the gardening store. Figure out the pattern to complete the chart.

Number of Flowers	1	2	3	4	5	6	7	8	9	10
Cost	$2	$4	$6	$8	$10		$14	$16	$18	

a. How much does it cost to buy 6 small flowers?

b. How much does it cost to buy 10 small flowers?

Peppers make a garden colorful. There are all kinds of peppers. Bell peppers can be yellow, green, or red. They look like bells. They do not taste very hot or spicy.

The banana pepper looks like a banana. You might think it is sweet. You would be right.

A garden plot is made up of peppers. This is the pattern for the first row of peppers.

a. What color will the 10th pepper plant be?

This is the pattern for the second row of peppers.

b. What color will the 10th pepper plant be?

Some **gardeners** plan their crops by season so they have food ready in the summer as well as in the fall. They plant zucchini for the summer. They plant acorn squash for the fall.

They also plant lots of pumpkins. Some will be just right for pies. One kind will be just right for jack-o-lanterns.

One family shares the garden work. They work out a plan for taking care of their garden.

Days	1	2	3	4	5	6	7	8	9	10	11
Kids	Miguel	Marie	Carlos	Miguel	Marie	Carlos	Miguel	Marie			

a. How many times does Miguel work in the first week?

b. Who will work on the 9th day?

c. Who will work on the 11th day?

Gardens are good for cities. They give people of all ages a place to work and to have fun. They can share the beauty of flowers and plants.

People may share the extra food that they grow. They can share the flowers, too. Best of all, people get to pick and eat what they grow!

Pumpkin Patch Profits

The community garden has many pumpkins. The gardeners make a pumpkin patch to sell the pumpkins. There are 45 small pumpkins. There are 10 large pumpkins. The money that the gardeners earn from selling the pumpkins will pay for next year's seeds and plants.

Pumpkins for Sale!

large pumpkins $5

small pumpkins $2

Solve It!

a. How much money can the gardeners make if they sell all of the small pumpkins?

b. How much money can the gardeners make if they sell all of the large pumpkins?

c. How much money can the gardeners make if they sell all of the pumpkins?

Use the steps below to help you solve the problems.

Step 1: Use a pattern to work out how much money the gardeners will make for selling 45 small pumpkins.

Total number of small pumpkins	5	10	15	20	25	30	35	40	45
Total profit	$10	$20	$30						

Step 2: Use a pattern to work out how much money the gardeners will make for selling 10 large pumpkins.

Total number of large pumpkins	1	2	3	4	5	6	7	8	9	10
Total profit	$5	$10	$15	$20	$25					

Step 3: Add the 2 totals to find out how much money will be made altogether.

Glossary

compost—rotted leaves and grass that are good for soil

crops—plants that farmers grow

drip irrigation system—a way to use less water and give water to plants using slow drips of water

gardener—a person who works in a garden

organize—to make a plan

pattern—something that repeats itself many times

plot—a portion of a garden

shed—a small building used for storing things such as rakes or shovels

Index

Let's Explore Math

Page 8:
a. bush
b. tree

Page 14:
a. red
b. gray

Page 19:
a. cabbage
b. broccoli

Page 21:
a. $12
b. $20

Page 23:
a. yellow
b. red

Page 25:
a. 3 times
b. Carlos
c. Marie

Solve the Problem

a. They will make $90 if they sell all of the small pumpkins.

Total number of small pumpkins	5	10	15	20	25	30	35	40	45
Total profit	$10	$20	$30	$40	$50	$60	$70	$80	$90

b. They will make $50 if they sell all of the large pumpkins.

Total number of large pumpkins	1	2	3	4	5	6	7	8	9	10
Total profit	$5	$10	$15	$20	$25	$30	$35	$40	$45	$50

c. If they sell all of the small and large pumpkins they will make $140 altogether.